BEATING BULLYING™

HOW TO BEAT PSYCHOLOGICAL BULLYING

JENNIFER LANDAU

rosen publishing's
rosen
central®

NEW YORK

Published in 2013 by The Rosen Publishing Group, Inc.
29 East 21st Street, New York, NY 10010

Library of Congress Cataloging-in-Publication Data

Landau, Jennifer, 1961–
How to beat psychological bullying/Jennifer Landau. — 1st ed.
    p. cm. — (Beating bullying)
Includes bibliographical references and index.
ISBN 978-1-4488-6809-4 (library binding) —
ISBN 978-1-4488-6815-5 (pbk.) —
ISBN 978-1-4488-6816-2 (6-pack)
1. Bullying—Juvenile literature. 2. Bullying—Prevention—Juvenile literature.
3. Psychological abuse—Prevention—Juvenile literature. I. Title.
BF637.B85L36 2013
302.34'3—dc23

                                                                2011041623

Manufactured in the United States of America

CPSIA Compliance Information: Batch #S12YA: For further information, contact Rosen Publishing, New York, New York, at
1-800-237-9932.

CONTENTS

Have you ever seen the way acid eats its way through metal? That is what psychological bullying does to its victim's self-esteem and sense of self-worth. Psychological bullies toy with their target's emotions, leaving him or her feeling ashamed, unworthy, and alone.

Some experts refer to this type of bullying as relational aggression. This means that the bully sets out to damage the victim's relationships with others by affecting how peers view that person. Psychological bullying affects how the target feels about himself or herself as well.

Psychological bullying goes far beyond a onetime snub in the cafeteria or a single dirty look in the hallway. It is a relentless attack that leaves the victims crushed and confused.

Examples of psychological bullying include the following:

- Spreading lies about a person or his or her family.
- Gossiping about someone with the intention of ruining his or her reputation.
- Holding one's nose or pretending to vomit every time the person walks by.
- Destroying the person's property on a regular basis: homework, lunch, or clothing.
- Threatening to beat someone up if he or she does not follow the bully's orders.
- Manipulating him or her by saying, "I won't be your friend if...."

Gossiping about someone in order to ruin her reputation is a type-of psychological bullying.

Some people may not take psychological bullying as seriously as other types of bullying. "Boys will be boys," they say, or it's just that "mean girl" phase that girls have to pass through on the way to adulthood. Psychological bullying can have devastating effects, though. It can lead to lifelong problems for all involved: the victims, the bullies, and even those who are bystanders to these attacks.

The Ophelia Project is an organization that studies relational aggression and works to support people who are bullied in this way. According to its research, 48 percent of students are regularly exposed to this type of bullying. Only 47 percent of students would report these acts, however, as opposed to 70 percent who would report physical bullying. While a black eye may be more dramatic than a broken spirit, it is misguided to view victims of psychological bullying as less in need of guidance.

This book will look at how it feels to be psychologically bullied and why certain teens are more likely to be targets than others. It also analyzes why teens bully, as well as what victims can do when a bully singles them out for abuse. Finally, it discusses what is being done on the local and national level to combat psychological bullying. While there are no quick fixes when it comes to such a complex problem, there are positive steps to take that can make a world of difference to an individual or community.

CHAPTER 1

SICK WITH WORRY

A victim of psychological bullying lives in a constant state of fear, wondering when the next strike will come. He or she feels helpless and depressed, unable to stop the mistreatment from a more powerful person. The bully may be older and physically stronger than the person being bullied, and likely more popular, too. The victim is so wounded that he or she begins to feel isolated from peers or family members.

Psychological bullying can be harder to spot than other types of bullying. No one is being beaten up or screamed at across the schoolyard. And much of this bullying takes place when teachers, parents, and other adults are not around to keep an eye on things.

According to a report by the Ophelia Project, 55 percent of students see psychological bullying—sometimes called relational aggression—during recess or break time, while 52 percent see this type of bullying in the cafeteria, and 42 percent see it in the hallways. At home or at the mall with a friend or a date, the person being bullied might feel even more alone.

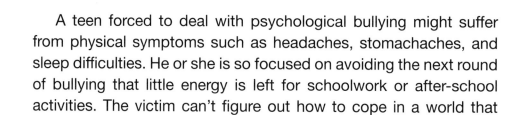

A teen who spends every day worrying about being bullied has little strength or attention left for coursework.

A teen forced to deal with psychological bullying might suffer from physical symptoms such as headaches, stomachaches, and sleep difficulties. He or she is so focused on avoiding the next round of bullying that little energy is left for schoolwork or after-school activities. The victim can't figure out how to cope in a world that often feels as if it's been turned upside down.

These feelings can lead to severe depression and anxiety as well as problems with alcohol or drugs. Some teens even commit suicide if they are unable to cope with the damaging effects of psychological bullying. The term "bullycide" is used to describe a person

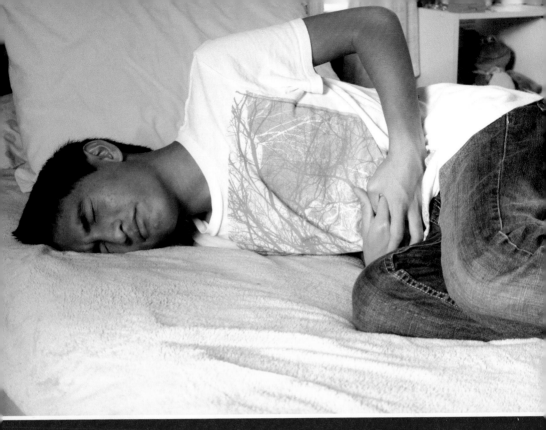

Psychological bullying can lead to physical symptoms such as head-aches, stomachaches, or trouble sleeping. Teens who are bullied might also experience depression and anxiety.

who is pushed to suicide by depression related to constant bullying. According to the Centers for Disease Control and Prevention (CDC), suicide is the third-leading cause of death for youths between the ages of ten and twenty-four. Although not all suicides can be directly related to bullying, this statistic is surely a cause for concern.

Some who have been bullied become so angry at how they are being treated that they rage against the bully or even against an entire group of people. Eric Harris and Dylan Klebold, two high school students who killed thirteen people at Columbine High School in Colorado in 1999, had been subjected to various types of bullying.

According to "Fighting Back," an article by Melissa Beattie-Moss in the online magazine Research/Penn State, Harris and Klebold recorded tapes in which Harris referred to being picked on about his face, hair, and shirts. Klebold warned the "stuck-up" kids that they would have to pay for the years of abuse he took from them. Clearly, there were many factors at play in the Columbine killings—Harris in particular was a very disturbed young man—but both teens did feel harassed by their peers.

The effects of being embarrassed, ignored, gossiped about, and threatened have long-term consequences. Some targets of bullying develop post-traumatic stress disorder (PTSD), an illness with symptoms such as overwhelming feelings of sadness, shame, guilt, and

BULLYING STUDENTS WITH DISABILITIES

A study in the *British Journal of Learning Support* stated that 60 percent of students with disabilities reported being bullied compared with 25 percent of the general school population. Psychological bullying of students who have disabilities includes acts such as pretending to be friends with someone and then making fun of that person in front of his or her peers. The bully might also convince the victim to do something that will get him or her in trouble at school or at home.

Some students, like those on the autism spectrum, have trouble reading facial cues or body language. This makes it hard for the person to recognize that he or she is being bullied, which only encourages more bullying. Other victims may get frustrated easily, have difficulty communicating, or exhibit other behaviors that mark them as "different" and lead to bullying.

hopelessness. These feelings can carry on into adulthood, affecting the victim's relationships with his or her spouse, coworkers, and friends.

A LIKELY TARGET

While almost anyone can be the target of bullies, it is those who look or act different who are most likely to come under attack. According to Do Something, Inc., a youth advocacy organization, most teens believe they are bullied because of their appearance or the size of their body.

Sadly, there are many reasons a teen might be bullied. A person who is considered a minority in a certain setting could be singled out. Examples of this include a Hispanic teen in a mostly white neighborhood or a girl who participates in an activity like skateboarding, which is usually done by boys.

A group of kids might follow the Hispanic teen after school, making him feel threatened. The bullies might demand money or spread rumors about the victim or his or her family. A girl participating in a mostly male sport could be subject to gossip about her sexual orientation based on nothing other than her love of that sport.

Teens who *are* lesbian, gay, bisexual, or transgender (LGBT) have a greater risk of being bullied. According to a 2009 survey by the Gay, Lesbian, and Straight Education Network (GLSEN), nearly two-thirds (61.1 percent) of LGBT students felt unsafe in their school because of their sexual orientation. Thirty percent of these students missed at least one day of school in the previous month because of safety concerns.

Several suicides by gay youths in 2010 brought more attention to the problem of bullying among this population. Although these teens are often the victim of a constant stream of antigay slurs, other forms of harassment are common. Psychological bullying of these teens includes obscene hand gestures, walking too close

A student returning to school after being homeschooled is one target of psychological bullies. This teen feels isolated from her peers and might lack friends to turn to when times get tough.

to the person in a way that feels threatening, or repeating mean-spirited gossip about his or her activities even when there's no proof that any of it is true. The LGBT teen begins to feel hunted at school and in the community. The victim may feel forced to hide his or her true self, adding to the psychological strain.

A teen returning to the school system after being homeschooled could be a target for bullies. Without a group of friends at school, he or she has fewer places to turn to for support. Someone with a slight stutter or a learning disability is frequently bullied. It is this vulnerability that the bully is after, something about a person that makes him or her seem less able to fight back once the attacks begin. This can also be a teen who spends a lot of time alone or one who is easily upset or rattled.

Sometimes one embarrassing moment is enough to get a bully going. Forget your line in the school play or trip in the hallway, and soon the bully is imitating your misstep or passing around a petition banning you from appearing in the next school play. The constant psychological bullying leaves you anxious and exhausted and wondering how you are going to make it through one more day.

CHAPTER 2

HOW BULLIES GAIN CONTROL

Teens bully because it makes them feel powerful and in control. They crave this feeling, almost as if it were a drug. Bullies always put their own needs first, and when these needs are not met, they grow impatient. Some bullies have been victims of bullying themselves. These bullies feel the need to act out a type of revenge for the poor treatment they've received from others.

Bullies are impulsive, too. They are quick to lash out when something doesn't go their way. That might mean sneering at a classmate as he walks down the hallway. In class, the bully might spend math period kicking a classmate's seat just hard enough to distract him. If the teacher notices, the bully stops. Then he hisses at his classmate as a warning when the teacher turns away.

At home, the bully might grab her little sister's lipstick and throw it down the toilet. In every case, the victim is caught off guard and left to wonder what's coming next. This gives the bully the high of power and control he or she was seeking.

A LACK OF EMPATHY

Most bullies lack any sense of empathy, which is the ability to look at a situation from someone else's point of view. Without empathy, there is little to control the bully's behavior. In fact, most bullies believe that their victims deserve to be treated badly. It's not the bully's fault that the other person isn't cool enough or athletic enough to earn respect.

Once a bully knows he or she has affected the victim, the bad behavior gets worse. Plots against the person being bullied become more elaborate. A bully steals a classmate's backpack and scrawls obscenities throughout the novel that's been assigned for class, knowing the book has to be returned soon. Perhaps a bully throws a party and invites a classmate, and then when he or she arrives, the partygoers act surprised that the person showed up. "Oh, inviting you over was a joke," the bully says. "Can't you even take a joke?"

THE POPULAR BULLY

There is a stereotype that bullies are unpopular people with low self-esteem. Through the school years, at least, the opposite seems to be true. Bullies tend to be popular, which is why they can draw others into their schemes. It is the cooperation of these bystanders that makes the bullies effective. It is also what makes those who are targeted feel as if they are constantly being ganged up on.

The victims are so isolated that they feel they have nowhere to turn. What can the victim do when his or her entire identity and social standing is in the hands of someone more powerful? At a time when a teen wants nothing more than to fit in, the effects can be devastating.

Bullies choose their targets carefully, picking someone who is already viewed as "different" by his or her peers. By going after a

As part of the Cartoon Network's Stop Bullying: Speak Up campaign, actors from *Dude, What Would Happen* show how helpless a bystander can feel when he sees someone being bullied.

person whose looks or dress or sexual orientation sets them apart, it is easier for the bully to get others to join in the bullying. If the bystanders don't join in, they are at least likely to look away.

The more a bully gets away with his or her behavior, the more it continues. In school, teachers are rarely in the hallways and lunchrooms where psychological bullying takes place. If they are, they may be too busy overseeing a large group of students to notice. Bullies count on adults being distracted and on their victims being

IT'S A GIRL THING

In the film *Mean Girls*, the character of Regina rules her high school. She decides who sits where, who wears what, and whether a classmate is worth talking to in the hallway. In her book *The Bully, the Bullied, and the Bystander*, Barbara Coloroso calls girls like Regina social bullies. While either gender can be a psychological bully, social bullies tend to be girls.

Interestingly, this is the group most likely to have poor self-esteem. A social bully deals with her bad feelings about herself by manipulating her so-called friend or cutting her victim off entirely, signaling her peers to do the same. Social bullies often come across as sweet and charming. Beneath that friendly mask, however, they are plotting their next move. Adults in particular have a hard time imagining that "good girls" could cause such harm. This makes it easy for social bullies to continue their nasty work.

too scared to speak up. A bully might even threaten the victim with a physical assault if she tells someone about what happened.

LEARNING TO BULLY

Bullies are made, not born. Somewhere along the way, bullies learn that acting out and terrifying others is a way to get what they want. Often these lessons begin at home.

Being a bully makes someone feel strong, but his or her family background is likely chaotic. One or both parents might be absent for long stretches of time. If not physically absent, the parents might pay little attention to their children. Children who are not given the proper emotional support from an adult have a greater chance of becoming bullies.

There is often some type of violence in the home. A parent might view screaming as the only way to gain some authority over the household. Parents might threaten to hit their children, creating an

Continually leaving someone out of group activities is another form of psychological bullying. These bullies control how others view their victim, destroying relationships and the target's self-esteem.

unbearable tension in the home. Drug and alcohol abuse might be a problem as well. When one parent is sick, the other is left to handle everything. If he or she snaps from the pressure, the children are the victims.

When a parent tries to gain control through bullying, the teen models that behavior because it is the only thing he or she knows. Sadly, the cycle continues as the teen begins to bully his or her siblings and peers.

Bullies are often brought up in a household that is chaotic and violent. They watch their parents act out and learn to do the same in order to get what they want.

THE DAMAGE DONE

It is clear that bullying takes a great toll on the victim. It affects his or her physical and mental health, perhaps for years to come. Bullying has a negative impact on bullies, too. As they get older, their popularity declines. Their peers mature, but bullies often don't. If they are still in school, their grades go down. They are more likely to abuse drugs and alcohol. Some may even join gangs.

Teens who bully often continue their behavior into adulthood. They bully others at work or at home. Criminal behavior might take place. According to researcher Dan Olweus, 60 percent of those who were bullies in grade six through nine had at least one criminal conviction by the age of twenty-four. Thirty-five to 40 percent of bullies had three or more convictions.

A study by Leonard Eron that spanned thirty-five years showed that childhood bullies become adults who have many unstable relationships. These adults spend a lot of time in family court dealing with issues of child custody and support. They also have high rates of alcoholism. Bullies may think they are strong and in control, but their behavior has a toxic effect on them as well as their victims.

MYTH Psychological bullying doesn't do any real harm. It's not like the victim is being punched or kicked.

FACT Psychological bullying causes great damage to the victim's feelings of self-worth. Depression and anxiety are common among victims, and they may even contemplate suicide. There are physical symptoms, too, such as headaches and stomachaches.

MYTH Psychological bullying is just a natural part of growing up.

FACT Psychological bullying may be common, but it is not natural. No one deserves to be treated poorly. Bullying should never be tolerated in any setting.

MYTH If you talk to someone about being bullied, you're just being a snitch.

FACT You're not being a snitch if you're trying to get yourself—or someone else—out of trouble. If your main interest is getting someone else into trouble, think about your motives before going forward.

CHAPTER 3

TAKING BACK YOUR POWER

Psychological bullying can crush your self-esteem to the point where you feel like you deserve to be abused. That is just the bullied, beaten-down part of you talking. The part of you that feels powerless to change your situation.

The truth is, you have done nothing to deserve being bullied. There are actions you can take to make your situation better, however. These are not miracle cures but steps toward making each day something to look forward to instead of dreading. No matter what steps you follow, always remember that your safety comes first. Never put yourself in a situation where your physical well-being is at risk.

It's important to remember that bullies feed off of the reaction they get from their victims. That's what keeps them coming back to bully some more. In her book *Bully Blocking: Six Secrets to Help Children Deal with Teasing and Bullying*, Evelyn Field uses the phrase "Don't show your pain for the bully's gain." This means that you should try to stay as calm as possible when a bully chooses you as a target. Without your strong reaction, the bully is not getting the jolt of power he or she craves. He or she might decide that it's not worth the effort to harass you.

Staying calm is easier said than done, of course. When a bully is threatening to spread some lie about you if you don't give him $5, it's hard to keep your cool. If the threat is to beat you up, walk away immediately. Report these threats to a trusted adult.

If you can, buddy up with other people when you're in areas like the hallway or lunchroom where you're likely to be bullied. There's less chance a bully will target you when you're in a group.

Students in this workshop learn to defeat bullies by boosting their self-esteem. In one exercise, they will themselves to hold their arms out in front even after they feel tired.

POWER SURGE

There are ways to make yourself feel stronger when confronted by a bully. Evelyn Field talks about "anchors," which can be anything that makes you feel empowered in stressful situations. Often these are objects such as religious symbols or jewelry or a token with a special saying on it. If a bully tries to bother you, touch a hand to this object. This will help you feel connected to something larger than your present situation. If it can help you appear unaffected by the bully's actions, the object has done its job.

Students work on building confidence by looking in a mirror and talking about themselves in terms that go beyond surface descriptions to something deeper and more unique.

Positive self-talk is also a very important tool. When a bully tries to push your buttons, picture yourself as someone who is strong and can handle the tough times. Say to yourself: "I am a good person. I deserve to be treated with respect. This is the bully's problem, not mine. I will not let him get to me."

Make sure your body language matches your actions. Maintaining good posture, keeping your voice steady, and your eye contact consistent will help you come across as confident.

If you feel as if you want to say something to the bully, make it short. You can simply disagree with what he or she is doing by saying, "I don't think so" or "That's not right." Never say, "You're a terrible person" or "You only bully me because I get better grades than you" or anything that could egg the bully on to worse behavior.

MANAGING ANGRY FEELINGS

Being a victim of bullying can make anyone feel angry. While lashing out against the bully—or anyone—is a bad idea, there are things you can do to release some of that pressure. These include:

Exercise: Go for a walk or run, or play a game of catch with a sibling. It's a great mood booster.

Journaling: Write down whatever thoughts or feelings come to mind, whether negative or positive. By releasing these emotions onto paper, they'll be less likely to build up inside.

Deep Breathing: If you feel like your heart is racing, take a moment to focus on your breath. Think of your abdomen as a balloon that you fill when you slowly breathe in through your nose. When you breathe out, the balloon deflates. Try to practice these deep, cleansing breaths every day.

PUTTING YOURSELF FIRST

If ignoring the bully or speaking your mind doesn't make things better, seek help from an adult. This could be a parent, teacher, coach, or guidance counselor. The important thing is to make sure that this person takes your concerns seriously. If he or she dismisses psychological bullying as "just what kids do," find someone else to help you. Try to keep a record of the different times when you've been bullied so that it's right there in black

If you talk to an adult about being bullied, make sure that he or she understands your concerns and takes them seriously.

and white. Let the adult know what you've tried so far to make things better.

Unfortunately, your problems with bullying will probably not go away overnight. While you work on long-term solutions, don't forget to take care of yourself. Sleep enough, eat well, and do something fun. Read a book in your favorite series. Go to the mall with a friend. Have a movie or video game night at home. This might be the right time to join a volunteer organization. You'll meet new people and feel good about working toward a common goal.

THE POWER OF THE BYSTANDER

Bullies feed off the reaction of not only their victims but also of bystanders. If a bystander—or group of bystanders—doesn't support the bully, he or she will lose a great deal of power. Yet according to a study by D. J. Pepler and W. M. Craig, bystanders reinforced what the bully was doing in 81 percent of cases, showing more respect toward the bully than his or her targets. In 48 percent of the cases, they were active participants in the bullying. Only 13 percent of the time did bystanders try to prevent the bullying from taking place.

Why are bystanders willing to go along with this cruel behavior? Perhaps they are afraid of becoming targets themselves. They might worry that trying to stop the bullying will make things worse for the victim. It could be that they simply have no idea how to help the victim.

Bullying has negative effects for both victims and bullies. Bystanders face consequences, too. They might feel guilty about refusing to help or become depressed about what they see as their own lack of character. In time, they might become less sensitive to another person's pain, making it hard for them to maintain relationships.

It's important for communities to show support for those who have been bullied. These teens are participating in an antibullying walk in Havre, Montana.

Bystanders can have a positive impact, however. They can refuse to join in the bullying or even watch it take place. They can approach the victim and let him or her know how sorry they are about what happened. Another idea is to talk to a school administrator or community leader about becoming an active part of any antibullying program. All these steps will help both bystanders and victims escape the devastating effects of bullying.

10 GREAT QUESTIONS

TO ASK A GUIDANCE COUNSELOR

1 My best friend's brother keeps looking at my body in a way that makes me uncomfortable. Should I talk to the brother about it or approach my friend first?

2 When I sit down to eat lunch, the kid across from me puffs out his cheeks to show me that he thinks I'm fat. Every time I move, he moves with me. What should I do?

3 This student in my gym class says he'll beat me up if I don't bring him $20. Yesterday he started following me home. How do I protect myself from his threats?

4 My friend got invited to a party, but I think it was a mean joke and he'll be asked to leave when he shows up. How do I tell him this without ruining our friendship?

5 These kids in my class keep pretending that they can't see or hear me because I'm small. I'm fed up. How can I get this to end?

6 This boy keeps warning me that if I don't go out with him, he'll tell everyone that I have a sexually transmitted disease. What will it take for him to leave me alone?

7 Why should I stick up for some student I don't know when he's being bullied? Who says he would do the same for me?

8 A girl who I thought was my friend suddenly stopped talking to me. Now a whole group of girls is doing the same thing. How do I stop them from treating me this way?

9 My older brother keeps taking my lunch money out of my backpack. How can I fix this without getting my brother really mad at me?

10 Someone keeps putting nasty notes in my locker. I can't tell who is doing it because the handwriting is not all the same. How should I handle this?

CHAPTER 4

ENDING THE VICIOUS CYCLE

On September 19, 2010, Dharun Ravi, a freshman at Rutgers University, went into a friend's room and set up a live Webcast of his roommate Tyler Clementi's romantic encounter with another man. This encounter soon became the subject of gossip in Clementi and Ravi's dormitory.

Ravi tried to tape Clementi again on September 21, daring his friends to video chat him between the hours of 9:30 PM and midnight. "Yes," Ravi wrote, according to the *New York Times*. "It's happening again." On September 22, 2010, Clementi, who was eighteen years old, jumped off the George Washington Bridge into the Hudson River, an apparent suicide.

The Clementi case has become famous as an example of cyberbullying and gay bashing. Dharun Ravi was charged with fifteen criminal counts for his actions, including bias crimes. These are crimes against a specific group of people, based on their race, or in Clementi's case, his sexual orientation.

There is no doubt that Tyler Clementi was the victim of cyberbullying and gay bashing. He was also the victim of psychological bullying. Imagine how humiliated Clementi must have felt by his

On October 3, 2010, people held a vigil for Tyler Clementi at Rutgers University. Clementi apparently killed himself after being a target of psychological bullying and gay bashing.

roommate broadcasting such a private act over the Internet fact, one of the charges against Dharun Ravi is invasion of priv. although he pled "not guilty" to all charges against him in May 2(In 2012, a jury found Ravi guilty of invasion of privacy, among o charges.

A TOUGH ISSUE TO TACKLE

News of Tyler Clementi's death came on the same day that Rutg University began a campus-wide campaign called Project Civ The project was meant to teach the importance of being kind respectful toward one another, with a particular focus on n technology such as the Internet. Sadly, Dharun Ravi is not the only one who finds these lessons difficult to learn. Bullying remains at epidemic levels throughout U.S. society.

President Barack Obama spoke about his concerns on March 10, 2011, at a White House conference on bullying: "If there's one goal of this conference, it's to dispel the myth that bullying is just a harmless rite of passage or an inevitable part of growing up. It's not."

Some view psychological bullying as "just" pranks or jokes that will toughen young people up for life in the real world. Yet, we have seen the damage that this type of bullying can do to everyone involved. That is what makes President Obama's comments so essential at this particular point in time.

COMMUNITY INVOLVEMENT

At the White House conference, First Lady Michelle Obama emphasized the importance of getting an entire community involved in the fight against bullying. She said that children need their parents' support and guidance when times get tough, but added, "[We] all need to play a role—as teachers, coaches, as faith leaders, elected officials, and anyone who's involved in our children's lives."

In September 2011, U.S. Department of Education secretary Arne Duncan hosted the second annual Bullying Prevention Summit. This two-day summit highlighted the efforts of both governmental and nongovernmental agencies to prevent bullying "in every way possible," Duncan said in a Department of Education press release.

The Department of Education has partnered with eight other federal agencies to deal with the challenges surrounding bullying. This campaign includes hosting Webinars on a wide range of topics related to the problem, as well as developing a consistent definition of bullying and analyzing how well current antibullying laws are working.

U.S. Education Secretary Arne Duncan poses with two students at the first federal Bullying Prevention Summit, which took place on August 11, 2010.

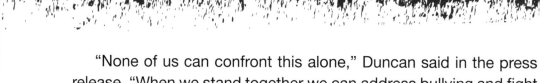

"None of us can confront this alone," Duncan said in the press release. "When we stand together we can address bullying and fight the hatred, bigotry, and fear that divide us. Our children deserve a chance. We must support them."

Many resources already exist within the community. These include mental health, education, law enforcement, and faith-based organizations. These groups can partner to find out the needs of the community and then work to coordinate antibullying programs.

Communities can determine their needs by using methods such as surveys, focus groups, and interviews. Questions to ask include the following:

- What types of bullying are people most concerned about?
- Is there a program already in place in the community to address these issues?
- If so, is it working?
- What makes it successful or unsuccessful?

Make sure that psychological bullying is included in the mix. It may not seem as dramatic as some other types of bullying, but it can be just as destructive. Listening to the thoughts and opinions of young people is also important. They are the ones dealing with these issues on a firsthand basis. In addition, raising community awareness should be part of any antibullying campaign. All forms of media—print material, TV or radio spots, Web sites—need to be included to reach as many people as possible.

With a problem as widespread and varied as bullying, no program is ever complete. There is a need for continued monitoring and intervention to stay on top of the concerns of the community.

CUTTING DOWN ON GOSSIP

A study published in *School Psychology Review* showed that using an anti-bullying program can cut down on malicious, or mean-spirited, gossip. The study was led by the University of Washington and took place at six elementary schools in the Seattle, Washington, area. After a three-month trial of an antibullying program, this type of hurtful gossip was reduced by 72 percent.

Once each week, researchers recorded the behavior of third- to sixth-graders during five minutes of playground time. The observations took place for ten weeks in the fall and ten weeks in the spring. Between the fall and spring, half of the thirty-six classrooms in the study took part in the anti-bullying program. By spring, students took who part in the program had 234 fewer instances of gossip per class of twenty-five. These were students who had gossiped before, so the decrease was substantial.

SCHOOL RULES

Schools are hotspots for all types of bullying, including psychological bullying. For any antibullying program to be effective, every adult in the building must be committed to its success. This begins with educating them about what to look for when it comes to bullying and how to handle each situation.

Most schools have codes of conduct in place. Among other things, these codes explain what consequences a student faces if he or she behaves in an unacceptable manner toward another student. These codes must be followed consistently or else no one in the school will take them seriously.

The culture of the school makes a huge difference. Authors Larry Brendtro and Nicholas Long talk about the four A's that safe and caring schools need to have in place:

Attachment: Helping students form close social bonds with each other and with teachers so that every student feels heard and supported

Achievement: Having high expectations for students, both in academic work and personal behavior

Autonomy: Encouraging students to take responsibility for their actions, rather than relying solely on discipline

Altruism: Developing a sense of self-worth in the student population by having them help others

By creating a supportive and positive school environment, students learn to be good citizens who don't need to tear others down to feel good about themselves.

ANTIBULLYING LEGISLATION

The Tyler Clementi tragedy did result in New Jersey passing the Anti-Bullying Bill of Rights, the nation's toughest law against bullying and harassment in the country. The law, which went into effect on

September 1, 2011, applies to public schools, and parts of the bill apply to public colleges as well. The bill requires that every school increase staff training and have a point person for addressing accusations of bullying. In addition, there are tight deadlines for reporting and investigating bullying incidents.

Beginning to put such a wide-ranging policy into place has proven difficult for some school administrators. They support the spirit of the law but feel that they don't have the resources or personnel to follow through. "I think this has gone well overboard," Richard G.

Members of Garden State Equality gathered in 2010 to support tougher antibullying laws for New Jersey. The organization champions civil rights and equality for lesbian, gay, bisexual, and transgender people.

35

Bozza, executive director of the New Jersey Association of School Administrators, told a reporter for the *New York Times*. Only time will tell whether this policy can be carried out effectively and reduce bullying in New Jersey schools.

Most states have some type of law against bullying. On the national level, two bills were introduced to Congress in the spring of 2011. The Safe Schools Improvement Act of 2011 (S. 506) would modify an existing bill to include specific language about policies related to bullying and harassment. The Successful, Safe, and Healthy Students Act of 2011 (S. 919) deals with both physical and mental health issues, but does talk about programs and strategies to prevent harassment, including bullying. As of the fall of 2011, both bills were in the early stages of the legislative process.

TAKING THE LONG VIEW

Every day there seems to be another story about someone being bullied to the point of hopelessness—or even suicide—because he or she is viewed as different. Some of these stories make the head-lines while many others are only discussed at the local coffee shop or while sitting around the dinner table.

While a bully may target a single individual, the poison aimed at one person affects many, including the bully. Only by working to change the culture that allows such acts to take place can a school or community hope to see lasting improvement. All types of bully-ing must be taken seriously. All members of a community must get involved to fight against this destructive practice. Naming one par-ticular week an antibullying week or coming up with a catchy slogan is a great way to raise awareness. However, it is a sustained effort to both discourage bullying and encourage tolerance and respect for all individuals that will have the most lasting impact.

abuse To harm someone or to treat someone with cruelty.

accusations Charges that someone has done something wrong or illegal.

advocacy Public support of a policy, cause, or group of people.

altruism An unselfish concern for the welfare of others.

autonomy Freedom to determine one's own actions and behavior.

body language The use of the body, rather than through speaking, to show feelings. Body language includes gestures, posture, and facial expressions.

chaotic In a state of confusion and disorder.

comprehensive Covering a wide range of content about a particular topic.

cyberbullying Using cellphones, e-mail, social networking, or other technology to bully someone.

depression A feeling of extreme sadness or gloom that lasts more than a few days.

devastating Highly destructive or damaging.

elaborate Worked out with great care and detail.

harassment The creation of an uncomfortable or hostile situation through words or actions.

impulsive Doing something without giving any thought to the consequences of your actions.

intervention The act of getting involved in a situation in order to change the outcome.

legislative Having to do with the writing and passing of laws.

minority A group of people that is different from the majority in terms of race, religion, ethnic background, or sexual orientation.

monitor To keep close watch on the progress of something over an extended period of time.

obscenities Words that are extremely rude and impolite. Obscenities are often intended to shock or offend.

personnel A group of people employed at the same place of business.

relational aggression Any behavior that is intended to harm someone by affecting his or her relationships with other people.

relentless Nonstop or never ending.

resource A source of supplies, support, or aid that can be drawn upon when needed.

self-esteem The degree to which you value yourself and your achievements. People with high self-esteem believe they deserve to be treated with kindness and respect.

sexual orientation A pattern of emotional, romantic, or sexual attraction toward members of the same, opposite, or both sexes.

FOR MORE INFORMATION

Gay, Lesbian, and Straight Education Network (GLSEN)
90 Broad Street, 2nd Floor
New York, NY 10004
(212) 727-0135
Web site: http://www.glsen.org
The Gay, Lesbian, and Straight Education Network offers information
about how to protect homosexual students from bullying. A list
of thirty-five GLSEN chapters is provided.

National Crime Prevention Council
2345 Crystal Drive, Suite 500
Arlington, VA 22202
(202) 466-6272
Web site: http://www.ncpc.org/topics/bullying
The National Crime Prevention Council works to be the country's
leader in helping people keep themselves, their families, and
their communities safe from crime. The council offers lesson
plans, fact sheets, and other resources about bullying.

The Ophelia Project
718 Nevada Drive
Erie, PA 16505
(814) 456-5437
Web site: http://www.opheliaproject.org
The Ophelia Project provides tools, strategies, and solutions for
those dealing with nonphysical forms of aggression, such as
relational aggression.

Pacer's National Bullying Prevention Center
8161 Normandale Boulevard
Bloomington, MN 55437
(952) 838-9000
Web site: http://www.pacer.org/bullying
Pacer's National Bullying Prevention Center offers videos, down-
loads, classroom toolkits, and many other resources to help
prevent bullying.

Safe and Caring Schools and Communities
Barnett House, Suite 504
11010 142 Street
Edmonton, AB T5N 2R1
Canada
(780) 447-9487
Web site: http://www.sacsc.ca
Safe and Caring Schools and Communities is a not-for-profit
organization dedicated to violence prevention and character
education for children and youth.

Safe@School
Ontario Teacher's Foundation
1300 Yonge Street, Suite 200
Toronto, ON M4T 1X3
Canada
(800) 268-7061
Web site: http://www.safeatschool.ca

Safe@School offers resources such as teacher training, school-
based programs, and videos designed to create safe,
respectful, and healthy environments for students.

HOTLINES

Anti-Cyberbullying Hotline, Boston Public Health Commission
(617) 534-5050
Boys Town National Hotline (800) 448-3000
CrisisLink (888) 644-5886
Kids Help Hotline (Canada) (800) 668-6868
KUTO Crisis Help (888) 644-5886
National Suicide Hotline (800) 784-2433
National Suicide Prevention Lifeline (800) 273-8255
National Youth Crisis Hotline (800) 448-4663
TEEN LINE (800) 852-8336
Trevor Lifeline for Gay, Lesbian, and Bisexual Youth (866) 488-7386
24-Hour Addiction Helpline (877) 579-0078
Youth America Hotline (877) 968-8454

WEB SITES

Due to the changing nature of Internet links, Rosen Publishing has
developed an online list of Web sites related to the subject of this
book. This site is updated regularly. Please use this link to access
the list:

http://www.rosenlinks.com/beat/psyc

Asher, Jay. *Thirteen Reasons Why*. New York, NY: Razorbill Books/ Penguin Group, 2011.

Blanco, Jodee. *Please Stop Laughing at Us: One Survivor's Extraordinary Quest to Prevent School Bullying*. Dallas, TX: BenBella Books, 2008.

Brown, Jennifer. *Hate List*. New York, NY: Little, Brown Books for Young Readers, 2010.

Burton, Bonnie. *Girls Against Girls: Why We Are Mean to Each Other and How We Can Change*. Orlando, FL: Zest Books, 2009.

Clements, Andrew. *Troublemaker*. Illustrated by Mark Elliot. New York, NY: Atheneum, 2011.

Criswell, Patti Kelley. *Friends: Making Them and Keeping Them*. Middleton, WI: American Girl Publishing, 2006.

Davis, Stan, and Julia Davis. *Empowering Bystanders in Bullying Prevention*. Champaign, IL: Research Press, 2007.

Desetta, Al, and Educators for Social Responsibility. *The Courage to Be Yourself*. Minneapolis, MN: Free Spirit Publishing, 2005.

Drew, Naomi. *No Kidding About Bullying: 125 Ready-to-Use Activities to Help Kids Manage Anger, Resolve Conflicts, Build Empathy, and Get Along*. Minneapolis, MN: Free Spirit Publishing, 2010.

Field, Evelyn M. *Bully Blocking: Six Secrets to Help Children Deal with Teasing and Bullying*. Rev. ed. London, England: Jessica Kingsley Publishers, 2008.

Fox, Annie. *Real Friends vs. the Other Kind* (Middle School Confidential). Minneapolis, MN: Free Spirit Publishing, 2009.

Hipp, Earl. *Fighting Invisible Tigers*. Minneapolis, MN: Free Spirit Publishing, 2008.

Huegel, Kelly. *GLBTQ: The Survival Guide for Gay, Lesbian, Bisexual, Transgender, and Questioning Teens*. Minneapolis, MN: Free Spirit Publishing, 2011.

Humphrey, Sandra McLeod, and Brian Strassburg. *Hot Issues, Cool Choices: Facing Bullies, Peer Pressure, Popularity, and Put-Downs*. Amherst, NY: Prometheus Books, 2007.

Ludwig, Trudy. *Confessions of a Former Bully*. Berkeley, CA: Tricycle Press, 2010.

Peters, Julie Anne. *By the Time You Read This, I'll Be Dead*. New York, NY: Hyperion Books, 2011.

Phillips, Rick, John Linney, and Chris Pack. *Safe School Ambassadors: Harnessing Student Power to Stop Bullying and Violence*. Hoboken, NJ: Jossey-Bass/John Wiley & Sons, 2008.

Schab, Lisa. *Beyond the Blues: A Workbook to Help Teens Overcome Depression*. Oakland, CA: Instant Help Books/New Harbinger Publications, 2008.

Sprague, Susan. *Coping with Cliques: A Workbook to Help Girls Deal with Gossip, Put-Downs, Bullying, and Other Mean Behavior*. Oakland, CA: Instant Help Books/New Harbinger Publications, 2008.

Summers, Courtney. *Some Girls Are*. New York, NY: St. Martin's Griffin, 2010.

BIBLIOGRAPHY

Beane, Allan L. *Bullying Prevention for Schools: A Step-by-Step Guide to Implementing a Successful Anti-Bullying Program*. Hoboken, NJ: Jossey-Bass/John Wiley & Sons, 2009.

Beattie-Moss, Melissa. "Fighting Back." Research/Penn State, October 3, 2005. Retrieved November 10, 2011 (http://www.rps.psu.edu/bullies/index.html).

Brendtro, Larry, and Nicholas Long. "Breaking the Cycle of Conflict." *Educational Leadership*, Vol. 52, No. 5, February 1995, pp. 52–56.

Coloroso, Barbara. *The Bully, the Bullied, and the Bystander*. Updated ed. New York, NY: Harper Paperbacks, 2009.

Davis, Stan, and Julia Davis. *Schools Where Everyone Belongs: Practical Strategies for Reducing Bullying*. 2nd ed. Champaign, IL: Research Press, 2007.

Ellis, Deborah. *We Want You to Know: Kids Talk About Bullying*. Regina, SK, Canada: Coteau Books, 2010.

Foderaro, Lisa W. "Private Moment Made Public, Then a Fatal Jump." *New York Times*, September 29, 2010. Retrieved August 15, 2011 (http://query.nytimes.com/gst/fullpage.html?res=9B07E6D91638F933A0575AC0A9669D8B63&pagewanted=all).

Haber, Joel, and Jenna Glatzer. *Bullyproof Your Child for Life: Protect Your Child from Teasing, Taunting, and Bullying for Good*. New York, NY: Perigee Trade, 2007.

Hu, Winnie. "Bullying Law Puts New Jersey Schools on Spot." *New York Times*, August 30, 2011. Retrieved August 31, 2011 (http://www.nytimes.com/2011/08/31/nyregion/bullying-law-puts-new-jersey-schools-on-spot.html).

Human Rights Campaign. "Safe Schools Improvement Act."
Retrieved July 17, 2011 (http://www.hrc.org/issues/12142.htm).

Kohut, Margaret R. *The Complete Guide to Understanding, Controlling, and Stopping Bullies & Bullying: A Complete Guide for Teachers and Parents*. Ocala, FL: Atlantic Publishing Group, 2007.

Lee, Jesse. "President Obama & the First Lady at the White House Conference on Bullying Prevention." The White House Blog, March 10, 2011. Retrieved August 1, 2011 (http://www.whitehouse.gov/blog/2011/03/10/president-obama-first-lady-white-house-conference-bullying-prevention).

Lines, Dennis. *The Bullies: Understanding Bullies and Bullying*. London, England: Jessica Kingsley Publishers, 2008.

McElroy, Molly. "Anti-bullying Program Reduces Malicious Gossip on School Playgrounds." *UW Today*, January 3, 2011. Retrieved August 31, 2011 (http://www.washington.edu/news/articles/anti-bullying-program-reduces-malicious-gossip-on-school-playgrounds).

Pérez-Peña, Richard. "Christie Signs Tougher Law on Bullying in Schools." *New York Times*, January 6, 2011. Retrieved August 15, 2011 (http://www.nytimes.com/2011/01/07/nyregion/07bully.html).

Pérez-Peña, Richard, and Nate Schweber. "Roommate Is Arraigned in Rutgers Suicide Case." *New York Times*, May 23, 2011. Retrieved September 2, 2011 (http://www.nytimes.com/2011/05/24/nyregion/roommate-arraigned-in-rutgers-spy-suicide-case.html).

Rigby, Ken. *Children and Bullying: How Parents and Educators Can Reduce Bullying at School*. Malden, MA: Wiley-Blackwell, 2008.

Swearer, Susan M., Dorothy L. Espelage, and Scott A. Napolitano. *Bullying Prevention and Intervention: Realistic Strategies for Schools*. New York, NY: The Guilford Press, 2009.

U.S. Department of Education. "Federal Partners Celebrate Anti-Bullying Efforts and Pledge to Continue Work at Second Annual Bullying Prevention Summit." September 21, 2011. Retrieved September 27, 2011 (http://www.ed.gov/news/press-releases/federal-partners-celebrate-anti-bullying-efforts-and-pledge-continue-work-second).

U.S. Department of Health and Human Services. "Best Practices in Bullying Prevention and Intervention." Retrieved July 20, 2011 (http://www.stopbullying.gov/community/tip_sheets/best_practices.pdf).

U.S. Department of Health and Human Services. "Community-Based Bullying Prevention: Tips for Community Members." Retrieved July 20, 2011 (http://www.stopbullying.gov/community/tip_sheets/community_based_prevention.pdf).

INDEX

ABOUT THE AUTHOR

Jennifer Landau received her M.A. in creative writing from New York University and her M.S.T. in general and special education from Fordham University. An experienced editor, she has also published both fiction and nonfiction, including *The Right Words: Knowing What to Say and How to Say It*.

In addition to her work as a special education teacher, Landau has taught writing to high school students and senior citizens. She has a particular interest in expanding inclusion opportunities for special education students and teaching these students self-advocacy skills. When she is not writing, she enjoys reading and spending time outdoors with her young son.

PHOTO CREDITS

Cover © istockphoto.com/Aldo Murillo; cover, interior graphics © istockphoto.com/aleksandar velasevic; p. 5 © istockphoto.com/johnmootz; p. 8 altopress/Newscom; p. 9 © Maria Deseo/PhotoEdit; p. 12 Baerbel Schmidt/Stone/Getty Images; pp. 16, 27, 30, 35 © AP Images; p. 18 Digital Vision/Thinkstock; p. 19 iStockphoto/Thinkstock; pp. 22, 23 © Pat Vasquez-Cunningham/Albuquerque Journal/ZUMAPRESS.com; p. 25 © Bill Aron/PhotoEdit; p. 32 Chip Somodevilla/Getty Images.

Designer: Nicole Russo; Editor: Kathy Kuhtz Campbell;
Photo Researcher: Amy Feinberg